SILVER LININGS

blessings for shadow times

Trust your heart, dear child. Let Love's infinite mercy wash over you. Waiting is a precious gift, offering tender acceptance of the shadows. May the still small voice whisper you Home to be all you already are. Embrace this moment.

Joy Fry
Seattle, Washington
Sacred Order of Monks and Artists

by Maxine Shonk, OP

DEDICATION

This book of blessings
is dedicated to the
Spirituality Network
in thanksgiving for 25
years of dreaming and
to its founder Noreen
Malone, OP, whose
contemplative roots did
indeed seed its future.

ACKNOWLEDGEMENTS

In all my "digging and groping" for these shadow
blessings there are many individuals who have
been digging and groping with me along the
way. My blessing team, Becca Bass, Amanda
Cushing, Sandra Kerka, Melissa Turner-Rustin,
and Judy Unger, is truly blessed … and blessing to
me in their feedback, their encouragement, their
prayer, their hard work, and their community.
It is truly a work of love. I'm grateful as well to
my proofreaders, Mo Meuse, Joe Fowler, and
Marilyn Larkin, who took the time to make me
look and sound good. I am especially grateful
to so many people who have so graciously fed
me with their stories of how the blessings have
touched them and moved them to bless. All are
blessed and made holy in this process but none
more than I!

ABOUT THE AUTHOR

Maxine Shonk is a Dominican Sister of Peace living in Columbus, Ohio, and ministering as a spiritual director, retreat leader, author, and preacher. With 20 years' experience teaching in elementary, secondary, and higher education, she serves as adjunct professor at Ohio Dominican University. She is a board member for The Spirituality Network, Inc., where she was a pioneer. She is especially committed to the Network's Women to Women program, listening circles made up of women of diverse backgrounds, including homelessness, abuse, addiction, and oppression. She may be reached at maxineop@yahoo.com.

TO THE READER

Examining the title of this book of blessings you might guess that it would be a difficult one to write. It takes a good deal more digging and groping to find blessing in the shadows of one's life. After all, it's not the first place I would go to find blessing for my life. As a matter of fact, the shadow or the dark time is where I would rather not go at all ... but it is where I'm called to go. So dig and grope I must ... if I am to find the deepest gifts and choicest blessings available to me. It is in fact where we are all called.

We are all too familiar with experiences in our lives that seem to obscure God's goodness to us and in us. We find ourselves in those places of darkness in our lives that throw us into the shadows and make it difficult to see the way clearly. As we attempt to make our way through these "clouds of unknowing," we must look for the proverbial "silver linings" to give us hope and to keep us moving toward the light. Indeed our faith tells us that behind the clouds and in the dark times God remains ever faithful to us and is waiting with blessing and light ... if we ourselves can remain faithful to the journey (to the digging and groping). It is what the path from death to new life is all about.

It was the recognition of this universal and cyclical journey from death to life, from darkness to light, from shadow to blessing that gave birth to the Spirituality Network whose silver anniversary we celebrate and to whom this book is dedicated. Its logo speaks it and its history gives witness to it. The same parable that was used as the basis for the epigram of its written history, *Drawn to the Living Water*, is the parable that describes the journey that the blessings in this book require:

PARABLE OF THE WELL

The Kingdom of God
is like the woman
who cast her bucket into the well.

It sinks deep into the water.
The deeper it plunges,
the darker the waters become
until the bucket is surrounded in
a darkness
that is total and complete.

But surrounded by
this darkness
it gathers
the purest of water.

The woman must let the bucket
sink freely.
When it is time to bring it up
she labors and struggles
with the weight of it.

It takes a long time
to pull it up from the depths.
It requires patience and courage.
But when at last
she has completed her task
she rejoices
for hers is the purest of water
and the sweetest of refreshment.

She shares it joyfully with her family
and with all those who are thirsty
saying, "Look how I have been
blessed!"

So is the Kingdom of Heaven for all
those who seek compassion
and who can let go into the depths
with patience and courage.

I have found that one of the most profound biblical understandings of the word blessing is "to make holy or sacred." So to be blessed is to be made holy and sacred. This was precisely God's intent at our creation. "God blessed them … and saw that it was very good." And when we are the ones blessing, our intent must be the same: to see the other as holy and sacred, which frees them to bless in turn.

We can bless our very life in this way and make it holy. We can even look at the shadow times and pray "God bless my darkness" and make it sacred so that it might yield its blessing and make us holy in turn.

It is in this spirit that I offer this book of blessings to you. The blessings in this book are born of a trust that, even in the deepest darkness, God waits for us with sweet refreshment. May you be blessed and made holy by them and bless and make holy through them.

Blessing upon Blessing,

Maxine Shonk, O.P.

Maxine Shonk, OP, Dominican Sister of Peace

USING THESE BLESSINGS

It is amazing to me and brings me to my knees in gratitude whenever I hear the stories of how the Spirit has carried these blessings far and wide, bestowing grace and awareness. There are many creative ways people have found to bless one another with them. Visit http://blessinguponblessing.com to post/read various and creative uses for the blessings. As I have read and heard these many uses, several observations come to me that I pass on to you:

- Whenever possible allow the Spirit to surprise you with a spontaneous or random choosing of a blessing.

- There is some very profound power of blessing when it is read aloud to you or over you by another. Whenever possible try this way of receiving.

- Be as creative as you want to be with the blessings. The Spirituality Network (spiritnetwk@hotmail.com) is exploring ways to make additional formats available.

REVERENCE

resistance

May the God
who resides in your
resistance bless you with
an awareness of the truth in
you that holds you back. With God
may you hold that truth with gentleness
and without judgment until it slowly reveals the
place of God in you and shows you the way forward.
May yours be the hand and heart that hold the
resistance of others with reverence as God's truth is
revealed in them. May the God of REVERENCE bless
you.

UNDERSTANDING

struggle

May you be made holy
by the God who knows
you in your struggle. This
is the God who knows you well
and understands your crying need
to know. May you be willing to wrestle
with God, like Jacob before you, seeking always to
learn the ways of God. May you come away from the
mat with a deeper understanding and trust in what
it means to be faithful and may you be a faithful
companion to all those who struggle. May the God of
UNDERSTANDING bless you.

PATIENCE

May God be present
to you whenever you
are *angry*, energizing
you to discover divine truths
wherever they may be found. May
you discern the heart of your anger and
speak the words that give birth to positive change and
mutual growth while the rest falls away like chaff. May
you be a patient presence to others in their anger.
May the God who holds you in your anger, the God of
PATIENCE, bless you.

anger

STRENGTH

May God empower you in your *weakness*. May you find strength in the God who lifts you up when you feel deficient and breathes courage into your spirit when you are afraid. May you find strength in the love God has for you and may you grow into the very creation that God intended in breathing life into you. May you in turn encourage and strengthen the weak ones around you. May the God of STRENGTH bless you in your weakness.

weakness

UNITY

May you be made
holy when you feel
fragmented and pulled,
scattered and strewn in the
reality of your life. May God gather
you up into hands that knead and mold
all things together to work for good. May God hold
each piece of you and may you let each piece be
held by God as you are once again made whole by
unconditional love. May the God of UNITY, who holds
all things together, bless you.

fragmentation

CLARITY

May God enter into
all that *confuses* you
and holds you in unrest and
unknowing. May you be blessed
with the willingness to abide in
the confusion long enough to allow
God to be revealed there. May this God who, at the
beginning of time, brought beauty and order out of
chaos and darkness, bring you to a deep calm and a
holy understanding of divine purpose. May the God of
CLARITY bless you always.

FULLNESS

May God come to fill
your *emptiness* and the
places that yearn for meaning
and value. May you open your
heart to the God who created you
with unconditional love and breathed
divine purpose into your being, filling you with
treasure beyond measure. May you find this gifting
God waiting and yearning for you in your empty
places. May the God of FULLNESS bless you.

emptiness

7

CONTEMPLATION

cloudy days

May God make you
holy on *cloudy days*,
inviting you into the inner
spaces of your being, calling
you to reflect on your relationship
with the universe. Whether you find
sun or storm behind the clouds of the day, may your
reflection bring you to a profound respect for your
own place and purpose in the cosmos. May the God of
cloudy days, the God of CONTEMPLATION, bless you.

HEALING BALM

May God be soothing
ointment for all that is
hurting in you. May this
God cover you with healing
grace and presence as you are
nursed back to health. May the balm of
God's love bring you to a place of perspective on your
life while the pain and hurt take their proper place
in your experience. May this new perspective bring
understanding and wisdom into the lives of all those
who know hurt. May God, HEALING BALM of your life,
bless you.

hurt

9

TENDERNESS

tears

May God make you
holy in your *tears,*
whether tears of sadness,
joy, anger, or fear. May divine
compassion wash over you as you
pour yourself into God's presence. May
you experience the tenderness of God who knows you
through and through and holds you close. May you be
the one who catches the tears of all those who cry for
understanding. May the God of TENDERNESS become
known to you and bless you.

COMFORT

May you know the
presence of God when
you feel *threatened* by
forces within or without. May
you be blessed with the grace to
know the saving hand of God upholding
you in mind, heart, soul, and spirit. May you know
the loving arms of God holding you in confidence and
comfort as you stand in the places that threaten you.
May it be your faith and trust that invites those on the
path with you into the sure knowledge of "God with
us." May the God of COMFORT bless you.

threat

11

TOUCH

May God be with you
when you feel most
abandoned. May you find
God around the corner from
your perception and waiting to
embrace you with unconditional love.
May the nearness of this hidden God be revealed to
you in the hands and hearts of those who journey
with you. Then may your hand be extended to those
around you who are looking for the loving touch of
God. May the hand of God, the God of TOUCH, be
with you.

abandonment

COMPANIONSHIP

May God bless
you on *ordinary
days*, gracing you with
an awareness of the beauty
of everyday, the comfort of the
commonplace, and the awe of life as
usual. May you hear the invitation to new excitement
over the constancy of God's care for you and to
profound thanksgiving for God's faithful presence.
May the God of ordinary days, your COMPANION God,
bless you.

ordinary days

FAITHFULNESS

grief

May God who knows your *grief* bless you with the gradual awareness that there is no dying that cannot be transformed into life beyond imagining. May God rise and be revealed to you in your loss just as surely as the flower emerges from the dying seed and the butterfly from the abandoned cocoon. May this ever faithful God be with you and gently stir hope into your grieving. May the FAITHFUL God bless you.

ASSURANCE

May God seep into
your soul when you
are *without hope*. May
you be graced with a growing
awareness of God present to
you, holding you in your despair and
embracing you with light even as you long to see in
the darkness. May peace and confidence descend like
dew upon your desert places, and may you be the one
who brings light to others in their hopelessness. May
you be blessed by God's ASSURANCE of love and light.

hopelessness

TRUST

May you be blessed
by the God who knows
the places in you that find it
hard to change, when what
is familiar and comfortable begins
to shift in you. May you experience God's
understanding gaze and hear the gentle invitation to
see your life in new ways and to watch as God works
new wonders in you. May you trust God and become
whole and responsive. May your journey toward
trust light the path of those around you who have
become stubborn in their resolve. May the God of
TRUST bless you.

resistance to change

COURAGE

May God's hand in
yours see you through
every *fear*. May the onset
of fear be your signal to look
to God standing close to you.
May God's love be your shield and may
the whisper of God's "Be not afraid" drown out the
clamor of your misgivings and worries. May you know
courage and may you, in turn, be encouragement and
comfort to all those on your path who are afraid and
vulnerable. May the God of COURAGE bless you.

fear

CONSOLATION

dis-ease

May God make you
holy in your *dis-*
ease, in those places
that are uncomfortable and
disconcerting. May you experience
the wonder of God's consolation in all
that disturbs you and the soothing presence of God's
nurture in all that is unsettled about your life. As you
anchor yourself in the peace that only God can give,
may you be peace to all those in turmoil around you.
May the God of CONSOLATION bless you.

18

INTEGRITY

May God carry
you through times
of contradiction and
opposition. In those
times may you know the total
acceptance of the God who knows you.
May God open you gently to the realities that frighten
you and softly whisper in your ear the "truth that will
set you free." And may your opening invite those who
oppose you to discover their truth as well. May the
gentle God of INTEGRITY bless you.

opposition

NEW FIRE

ashes

May you be found
by God when your
path is obscured by the
ashes of your life. When the
contentment of the present is
disturbed and broken by the failures of
the past, may the God of beginning again become
known to you. When the ashes of what once was
threaten to cover you, may the God of New Fire fan
into flame the hidden embers that lie within. May this
rekindled energy light the way for others who walk
with you. May the God of NEW FIRE bless you.

UNCONDITIONAL LOVE

May God receive you
in your *vulnerability*.
In times of limitation may
you become susceptible to
God's care for you and overcome
with God's power in you. May you open
yourself totally to the unconditional love of the God
who created you and knows you perfectly in this
moment. In your own needy places may you learn
how to be in communion with the vulnerable ones
around you. May the God of UNCONDITIONAL LOVE
bless you.

vulnerability

JUSTICE

May God's spirit bless you when you see or experience *injustice*. May you be overtaken with a passion for truth as you guard and preserve your own integrity. May you stand *up* for those without voice, stand *in* for the victims of oppression and discrimination, and stand *out* in your persistence and desire for God's peace and justice in the world. May you live your life in pursuit of truth and in profound reverence for all of God's creation. May the God of JUSTICE bless you always.

injustice

IMAGINATION

May God awaken
you to a wider vision
when you become fixated
and absorbed in that which
does not last. May you exchange
the comfort of your *addictions*
for the anticipation of God's loving plan for your
happiness and peace. May the world that God
envisions captivate your attention and bring you to a
wholehearted pledge of faithfulness as you journey
toward God's dream. May that journey bear witness
to all who know you. May the God of IMAGINATION
bless you.

addiction

GOODNESS

shame

May God bless you
and make you holy in
those places of shame in
you where you want to hide
your face so you cannot be seen. In
those places may you experience God's
Spirit gently uncovering what is hidden, receiving all
of who you are and embracing it with love and mercy.
May God complete the incomplete in you so that she
might partner with you in bringing peace and healing
to the world. May you entrust yourself to this God,
this Spirit of GOODNESS, and may you be blessed all
your days.

RESILIENCE

May you be made holy
when you know *failure,*
when the object of your
dream eludes you or your hopes
dissolve in mistakes or shortfalls.
May you learn resilience in letting go and
hope in giving over to a God who knows you well and
loves you. May you know the eagerness of God to
embrace you and to guide you into fresh perspectives
and new ways to minister to those around you. May
you give yourself the gift of compassion and may the
God of RESILIENCE bless you.

failure

25

NONVIOLENCE

May you be
accompanied by God
when you encounter
violence. In times of hostility
may you be drawn deeply into
the stillness where God resides. In this
stillness may antagonism give way to cooperation,
resentment yield to forgiveness, and competition be
transformed by honor. May you bring this stillness to
all you meet and may you bless each one with peace.
May the God of NONVIOLENCE bless you.

violence

HEALTH

May you know the
blessing of health when
you experience *illness*.
May God wash over you with a
sense of well-being as you receive
the love and nurture of those around
you and the security of God's total care for you.
May you be restored to wholeness in mind, soul,
body, and spirit, and may comfort be yours as you
recover and reclaim the goodness with which you
were created. May the God of HEALTH be with you.

illness

27

REST

weariness

May God make you
holy when you are tired
and *weary,* when the work
of the day exhausts you or the
burden of life weighs upon you.
At these times may you be lifted into
Sabbath time with God, who rested after all the work
he had done and realized how good it all is. May
you look back on your day and on your life and see
goodness. May you rest in that goodness and know
God's blessing of REST.

FORGIVENESS

May God attend you in
times of *regret,* those
times when you look back
upon your day, your life, with
sorrow and "if only" on your lips.
May you experience God's understanding
gaze and hear the whisper of love. May God once and
for all relieve you of the burden of regret and replace
it with the freedom that comes with forgiveness. And
may your freed spirit be invitation to those around
you to choose and celebrate life. May the God of
FORGIVENESS bless you.

regret

ACCEPTANCE

May God bless you
when you become
paralyzed by unreal self-
expectations or by the
expectations of others. As
you tighten your fist around your many
"shoulds," may you experience God's loving touch
loosening your grip and opening you to a gentler
holding, to a place of self-compassion and acceptance.
In the opening may you love yourself as God loves you
and share that unconditional love with those around
you. May the God of ACCEPTANCE bless you.

expectation

NOW

May you be made
holy when you are
impatient. May God bless
you with the grace you need
to wait and watch for God's time.
May your need for results and answers
be transformed into vigilance for God's desire for you.
As you pass the time may you discover the God who
lingers with you in the unknown and is revealed in
the in-between times of your life. May the God of the
present moment, the God of NOW, bless you.

impatience

NEWNESS

disappointment

May God bless you
when you are plagued by
disappointment. When
what might have been fades
into disillusion and previously held
expectations seem foolish, may God
step into the breach with renewed vision and new
hope. May you look to this God to lead and guide
you through the mire of disenchantment and into the
fresh green meadows of God's vision and God's way
for you. May the God of NEWNESS bless you.

CONFIDENCE

May God bless you
in the times of your
ambivalence, when you
are unsure and indecisive. At
those moments may you reclaim
the unique truth God has planted deep
within you and is calling out of you. May you speak
with confidence and may you trust the word of
God in you that longs to have a voice. May your
confidence draw out truth from those around you.
May the God of CONFIDENCE bless you.

ambivalence

FAITHFULNESS

defeat

May you be blessed
when you are feeling
defeated and overcome by
circumstances in your life. In
those times may you be made holy
in your faithfulness. May you stand with
courage alongside God who positions God's self with
you and holds you in Love. May you look to that God
for the serenity that you seek and may that serenity
be your gift to those around you. May the God of
FAITHFULNESS bless you.

PROTECTIVE LOVE

May God bless you in
your frailty. When you
stand defenseless in a world
of domination and when your
spirit is naked and vulnerable to
forces beyond you, may you experience
the cloak of God gently placed around your shoulders.
May you be covered and protected by truth and
goodness, and may you be wrapped in a realization
of the power of God's immense love for the least
ones in and around you. May you be blessed by God's
PROTECTIVE LOVE.

frailty

HOPE

May you be made
holy when *depression*
descends like a fog, when
nothing can be seen clearly
and all things are wrapped in a
darkness out of which there seems no
path. From the cloud may God be for you a dim but
growing lamp of hope to accompany you. As you
navigate the darkness in the light of God's presence,
may you gradually and gently walk into a clearer day.
May the God of HOPE accompany you always and in
all ways.

depression

COMPLETION

May God bless the
one in you who is
dissatisfied and longs for
something more, the hungry
one who yearns for wholeness
and meaning. As you stand in the hungry
places, may you be in solidarity with all the hungry
ones around you. In your fidelity to your longing
may God be revealed as the one who fulfills your
greatest desire. May this be the God you introduce
to each one with whom you stand. May the God of
COMPLETION bless you and make you whole.

dissatisfaction

TRANQUILITY

anxiety

May God stay with
you when the demons of
anxiety surround you and
when worry interrupts your
peace and overtakes your trust.
May you experience the comforting hand
of God upon your trembling shoulder and know that
you are not alone in your concern. May you trust the
God who knows all things and holds all things and
makes all things work together for good. May you
entrust your cares to and may you be blessed by the
God of TRANQUILITY.

LIGHT

May you be made holy
in the shadows of your
life, in those unacknowledged
places that linger in the
periphery of your living and
are kept under the cover of darkness.
May the light of God's compassion guide you as you
withdraw your judgment of those places and discover
instead the hidden gifts of your life and the great
depth of your creation. Then may that light shine forth
from you to reveal the gifts hidden in those around
you. May the LIGHT of God bless you.

shadows

GOD WITHIN

resentment

May you be blessed
by God when you
begin to feel the pangs of
resentment or envy. In
those times may you open your
own heart and see the utter uniqueness
of your existence. May you see yourself as God sees
you ... beautifully and wonderfully made ... in God's
very image! May you see the eyes of God gazing back
at you with eternal pride and ever unconditional love.
May these be the eyes with which you gaze upon those
around you. May the GOD WITHIN be blessing for you.

EMPOWERMENT

May God be with you
and bless you when
you are feeling puny and
inadequate, when your
energy and resources are spent. At
those times may you know God breathing
life into all that you say and do, and may God's spirit
speak through you with amplified resonance to
those around you. For it is not you but God in you
who prays and moves and has being. May the God of
EMPOWERMENT bless you.

inadequacy

RE-CREATION

defilement

May God bless you
when you experience
yourself as *defiled* and
dirty, when you are marred and
damaged through abuse or trauma.
At those times may you remember that
it was from the dust of the earth that creation came
to be. It is from the dirt that seed comes to flower
and grain grows and feeds. May you experience the
soil from which you come not as dirty but as rich and
fertile in the hands of such an ingenious God. May
the God of RE-CREATION bless you.

MERCY

May God bless you in
times of betrayal when
you fall victim to duplicity or
pretense and your ability to
trust is diminished. At those times
may you and God together reach into
your heart-self and draw from a wider perspective.
May you see yourself as more than your hurt and
your betrayer as more than the offense. May God's
heart of mercy couple with your own as you live into
peace. May the God of MERCY bless you and restore
your trust.

betrayal

43

SOUL MATE

dying

May God accompany
you and bless you in
your times of *dying*. May
God walk with you into the
unknown as you say goodbye to
what is familiar and beloved. In this time
of letting go may you give yourself over to all that is
loving, life giving, and eternal and all that lives on in
memory and in mystery. May you be blessed by the
ones who know you and received by the One who
created you and has loved you from the beginning of
time. May God your SOUL MATE bless you.

PRESENCE

May you be blessed
and made holy when
you are *disheartened*
and demoralized by the forces
around you. At those times may
you be encircled and shielded by the
presence of God. May God's presence within you
awaken the place of your inner authority. And may
God's presence with you empower you to speak
your truth in love. May the PRESENCE of God bless
you always.

disheartenment

UNION

isolation

May you know God
is with you in your
isolation whether it is by
chance or by choice. When you
are feeling remote and distanced
from all else, when you stand alone
with no visible means of support, may you find the
God of union. May you discover this God in the small
crevices of your awareness, loving you just as you are
and inviting you to be one with yourself. And in that
reunion may you come into one with all creation. May
the God of UNION bless you.

LOVING CARE

May God make you holy when you find yourself *impoverished* and without means. When you experience a deprivation of your resources, may you look toward the source of your life and happiness. May you entrust yourself to God's provident care in the midst of your need, and may you be willing to be "reduced" to a life of thanksgiving as God tends to your every need. May God's LOVING CARE bless you.

impoverishment

47

LISTENING

May you be blessed by
God the listener when you
most *need to be heard* —
when you need to speak your
truth and your story and have it
received without condition or judgment.
May you know God's acceptance of how you are and
unconditional love for who you are in this moment.
May you discover the wisdom planted deep in your
own heart as God listens you into life and freedom.
May the LISTENING God bless you.

need to be heard

REASSURANCE

May the constancy of
God's reassurance bless
you when you are full of
doubt, when your questions
insist that life must make sense
and that good must follow reason. At
those times may you remember the mystery of
God's relationship with you: that God chose you
with love and not with logic, unconditionally and
without doubt. May God's REASSURING PRESENCE
with you and in you be blessing as you minister to all
those who live in doubt.

doubt

SAFETY

homelessness

May God bless you in your *homelessness*. When you find no place of ease, may God be your comfort. When a place of safety eludes you, may you find safe people surrounding you. When there is no place of calm in your weariness, may you rest in God's love and care for you. And may you become that home, that place of safety for all the "homeless" ones in your life. May the God of SAFETY bless you.

POWER

May you be made holy
in your *helplessness,*
when you must stand
powerless in the face of realities
that are not in your control. At
those times may you look around with
compassion for those who share your vulnerability,
and may you realize together that you need not stand
alone. May you know the reality of God's presence
and the mystery of God's power in your life. May the
POWER of God bless you.

helplessness

51

BLESSED SLUMBER

sleeplessness

May God be with you in your sleeplessness. May the thoughts and tensions on your mind or in your heart let go of you for a time and make room for peaceful slumber and refreshment. And may you let go into the heart of God all that concerns you and weighs upon you. Kept safely in God's care, may all be transformed into grace and blessing for your life. May the heart of God bring you BLESSED SLUMBER.

RESTFULNESS

May you be made
holy in the midst of your
restlessness. May God
enter into the place of your
agitation and focus you into a
place at the center of your being, the
place where what is scattered becomes connected
once again and all that is divided becomes whole. As
you experience this divine presence in you, may you
yourself become one with your creator and with all
creation around you. May the God of RESTFULNESS
bring you into wholeness and bless you with peace.

restlessness

CONSTANT COMPANION

May you be blessed with an awareness of God when you are *lonely*. When the "empty chair" looms large in your life and you long for relationship and connection, may you look for God who comes to sit with you ... in the guise of a child or the person in need or the neighbor who inquires. May you also find God in the reflection in your mirror — always inviting, always longing to be in relationship with you. May God, CONSTANT COMPANION, bless you always.

SERENITY

guilt

May you know God
with you when you are
experiencing feelings of
guilt. May your sense of
responsibility and accountability
be coupled with the gift of discernment
and truth. May the wisdom of God help you
to distinguish between the places of authentic
responsibility that bring you to growth and the places
of toxic guilt that drain you of truth. May you claim
all that is yours and let go of all that is not. May the
God of wisdom aid you in knowing the difference and
bless you with SERENITY.

ORDER

disorganization

May you be blessed
when you feel especially
disorganized, when the
disarray of your life overcomes
you and chaos reigns over your
day. In those times may you experience
God wading through with you and helping you discern
the pieces of your life that are important for your
fulfillment and happiness. Thus may you come to order
and peace, focused on the God who loves you and
accompanies you. May the God of ORDER bless you.

PEACE

stress

May God bless you
in the midst of tension
and stress, when nerves
are taut and the pressure to
succeed is high. May you stop and
experience the key of God's peace ever
so gently unwinding and releasing the tightness and
pressures of the day. May you rest in the knowledge
that God receives you just as you are and invites you
to do the same. God loves you beyond telling. May
this realization bring you into a place of tranquility and
self-care. May the God of all PEACE bless you.

INTUITION

May God bless you
when you are faced with
deafness or an inability to
hear. May you be comforted by
the God who hears you well and
listens to your every desire. May this God
help you to use your "inner ear" to hear the feelings and
thoughts of each person. May you listen with your heart
to what is not being said. May the God who knows all
work through you and bless you with a compassionate
heart. May the God of INTUITION bless you.

deafness

MYSTERY

May you be blessed
when you are forced
into the darkness of the
unknown, when answers
elude you and you are paralyzed
by anticipation or fear. At those times
may you hear yourself being called into the mystery
of God. May you entrust yourself into the hands
of mystery and know that you are not alone or
unprotected but loved and cared for. May the God of
MYSTERY bless you.

unknown

PERFECT LOVE

perfectionism

May God bless you
in your *need to be
perfect*. May the God of
perfect love be revealed to you
as the One who loves and accepts
you unconditionally just as you are. May
the God of perfect mercy embrace you and continually
re-create you even with your flaws and inadequacies.
May God transform your journey to perfection into
a journey toward God who is perfect lover and
companion. May the God of PERFECT LOVE bless you.

60

LOVING GOD

May God bless you when you are feeling *embarrassment*. May God embrace you in those awkward moments of your life that leave you uncomfortable and self-conscious. May you hear God's word of unconditional love and total acceptance whispered into your heart, and may you feel the arm of God holding you in your vulnerability. May God's belief in you move you to love and acceptance of those around you. May your LOVING GOD sustain and bless you.

embarrassment

DISCERNMENT

May God make you
holy as you endure
misunderstanding
and differences of opinion
with others. With God may you
step back from the fray in order to see
others as more than their dispute and to see the
whole of who you are in God's eyes. May this divine
perspective bring you to a place of discerning each
one's purpose and recognizing each one's integrity as
you seek resolution. May the God of DISCERNMENT
bless you.

misunderstanding

BALANCE

May God bring you
blessing when you find
yourself *compulsed* and
driven by inner forces that
want to bypass virtue in favor
of outcome. May God's presence in
you temper your passion with patience and
compassion. May you know that God stands with
you in all your efforts and guides you with a loving
hand to all that is good. May the God of BALANCE
accompany you all your days.

compulsion

REFLECTION

reluctance

May God bless you
when you are *reluctant*
to respond to what is asked
of you. May God grant you a
reflective heart as you honor your
hesitation. May you be given a heart that
is both alert to your inner needs and courageous in
serving the needs of those around you. May you be
blessed with a discerning heart as you respond in
love to God's invitation. May the God of REFLECTION
make you holy.

GRACE

May you be made
holy when you are
overwhelmed by worry or
work or bent over by demands
on your life. May God ease your
overwhelm with the touch of grace on
your spirit, calling you to partake of each moment,
appreciating the present, and the presence, of
those around you. May you stand up straight with
a profound awareness of God's grace and life
within you. May God's GRACE be upon you.

overwhelm

RESOURCEFULNESS

obstacles

May God be with you
and bless you when
you find yourself faced with
obstacles in the road of life,
barriers that block a straight path
to wholeness, accumulations of others'
making or of your own. May God help you to know
when to work through the obstacles and when to
go around them. May you always have as your goal
the wholeness of all creation and oneness with the
Creator. May the God of RESOURCEFULNESS bless you.

SILENCE

May you know the
protection of God when
panic and terror strike you.
When you experience dread
and the paralysis of not knowing,
may you feel the strong arm of God gently
enfolding you in a safe embrace. May this God calm
your fears and whisper words of comfort into your
ear, bringing you to a tranquil and sure knowledge
of Divine Presence with you and in you. May the
God of SILENCE bless you.

panic

WAKEFULNESS

boredom

May you be made holy when you are experiencing boredom or monotony and are bothered by the sameness of the everyday. At those times may God alert you to the tiny surprises: the smile of an infant, the concert sounds of nature, or the sweet taste of the perfect cup of tea. In noticing these "God insertions" may you come to know an excitement for the everyday revelations of God's unbounded love. May the God of WAKEFULNESS bless you.

VISION

May God bless you
in your *blindness*.
When it is impossible to see
in spite of all your looking,
may God bless you with the
ability to envision a better world and
to visualize a healed creation. May you be given
the gift of prophecy as you share your vision with
all who surround you. And may you help others to
see by your touch of compassion and your word of
encouragement. May the God of VISION bless you.

blindness

69

AWAKENING

May you be especially blessed by God in times of loss. In your letting go of the past, a relationship, health, youth, or any loss, may you take the time to remember and to reflect on how the object of your loss has gifted you and what has been awakened in you as a result of its presence in your life. Then may yours be a grateful goodbye to what was, so that you may say a gracious hello to the "more" that God holds out to you. May the God of AWAKENING bless you.

SUPPORT

May you be made holy
when you are *crippled*
and cannot stand on your
own. When it is difficult to
move, may God take you into
the places of the heart where God
wishes you to be. Supported by God, may you
know yourself to be carried and cared for with
unconditional love and undivided attention. And
may you drink in the goodness of such a God who
has hold of you. May God Your SUPPORT bless you.

crippling

WHISPER OF GOD'S PRESENCE

speechlessness

May God bring you blessing when you find yourself speechless and inarticulate, when you stand mute in the face of your reality. At those times may you know the presence of God within you, the wordless whisper of God's love and care for you. With Elijah may you hear that tiny whispering sound that speaks God's presence and empowers you to give voice to truth. May the WHISPER OF GOD'S PRESENCE bless you.

BENEVOLENCE

May God bless
you when you find it
impossible to forgive
another. When you cannot find
it in your heart, may you know
that true forgiveness is found in the heart
of God ... that God receives you first in your desire
to forgive. May you go to the God who forgives you
and learn the meaning of mercy. Then may you trust
God to gradually and gently bring you to forgiveness
of others. May the BENEVOLENT God bless you and
make you holy.

unforgiveness of others

73

APPRECIATION

aging

May you be blessed
as you engage the
aging process. As the
years gather your wisdom,
may you be graced with gratitude
for your life. May you experience God's
loving embrace and gratitude for your faithfulness
to the journey, and may you be blessed with new
appreciation of your call to be at one with all
those who have peopled your life. May the God of
APPRECIATION bless you all your days.

PERSPECTIVE

May you be made holy
when you are feeling
frustrated and at wit's
end. When words fail your
understanding and actions yield no
results, may you step away with God for
that moment of silence that brings clarity. May you
be given the perspective of a broader purpose and
a wider vision. May you see as God sees and be
redirected toward what is good and true. May the
God of PERSPECTIVE bless you.

frustration

WHOLENESS

comparison

May God be with you
and bless you when you
begin to *compare* yourself
with others in your effort
to become whole. May you be
blessed with the awareness that you were
whole at your creation and God awaits your return to
your true self. Trusting in this God, may you no longer
be fragmented and exiled by your need to compare
but drawn into fullness by the promise of your own
homecoming. May the God of WHOLENESS bless you.

CARE

May God stand with
you when you are
devastated by tragedy
or circumstance. When you
become paralyzed by your reality,
may God catch you in arms of tenderness
and hold you with unwavering love. May you be
stilled and quieted by the realization that God will
never let you go or abandon you. May you know
the blessing of God's CARE for you.

devastation

HONOR

exclusion

May you be blessed by
the God who knows you
and loves you when you feel
separated and *excluded* from
your surroundings and overlooked
by those around you. May you honor the
truth of your own being and be willing to stand in it
... even when you must stand alone. As you search
for the "truth within you," may you discover "God
within you" and know them to be one and the same
and that you are never really alone. May the God of
HONOR bless you.

SELF-COMPASSION

May God bless you when you are *unable to forgive yourself*. At such times may you look upon yourself with the eyes of God and learn self-compassion. May your mercy toward yourself be modeled on God's mercy toward you ... undeserved yet given. With the eyes of God may you see yourself as limited yet loved unconditionally, bound by love yet freed to love and to proclaim God's goodness in and to all of creation. May the God of SELF-COMPASSION bless you.

unforgiveness of self

SELF-ACCEPTANCE

marginalization

May God bless
you when you are
in the *margins* and
in the minority. When you
find yourself dominated and
outnumbered, may you know that God
accepts you and counts you as a treasure. May you
stand out in your uniqueness, in your compassion,
and in your giftedness as God's beloved. May God
bless you with faithfulness to your truth and the
fullness of love. May the God of SELF-ACCEPTANCE
bless you.

ENTRUSTMENT

May you be blessed
when you are caught
up in the *messiness* of
life, when the daily directions
begin to go this way and that
and nothing seems to follow the
pattern you've set. At those times may you know
the freedom to let go of your plan and, with a
discerning heart, to watch for God's design in your
life. May you trust in the chaos knowing that it was
from such that the world came to be. May the God
of ENTRUSTMENT bless you.

messiness

81

CLEAR VISION

apprehensiveness

May you know blessing when you are feeling *apprehensive* about many things and anxiety blocks the vision of your life. At those times may you recall that *God's* vision for you remains steadfast and clear, that you are held on a steady course toward the very heart of God. May this remembering bring you back to a place of peace, a place of letting go and letting God guide your life. May this God of CLEAR VISION bless you.

STILLNESS

May the God of
stillness bless you
when you find yourself
competing with others, or
with God, for pride of place. May
you recognize in God's unconditional love
for you that there is already a place for you, assigned
at your creation, which only you can fill and only your
gifts can bring to fullness. In the still places of your life
may you recognize and claim that place and come to
wholeness in it. May the God of STILLNESS bless you.

competitiveness

ABIDING PRESENCE

inertia

May God make you holy when you feel stalled and stuck and nothing seems to motivate you or move you forward in your journey. In these neutral places may you imagine God coming to rest beside you, grateful for the time to be with you in the idleness. May you take this time to notice where you are and to listen for the voices in your environment or within your heart. And may you experience the wordless presence of God in the quiet places. May the God of ABIDING PRESENCE be with you.

SELF-KNOWLEDGE

May God bless you in times of *insensitivity*. When you become aware of your lack of attention and thought for those who call out to you, may you be blessed with the wisdom to discern and recognize the thoughts that preoccupy you, the courage to examine them and the grace to address them. Through this inner journey may you return then to being a compassionate presence to God's people. May our Gracious God bless you with SELF-KNOWLEDGE.

insensitivity

PROMISE

sadness

May you be made
holy when you become
saddened by the reality
around you. May you be
brought to the realization that
God weeps and is troubled when you are
troubled, concerned when you are concerned. May
you realize also that God is compassionate when you
are compassionate and gentle when you are gentle
with the sorrows of another. May you be blessed in the
knowledge that God's presence is experienced through
you. May the God of PROMISE bless you.

VITALITY

May God make you
holy when you feel
numb and immobile,
paralyzed by fear or anxiety,
anesthetized by compulsion or
trauma. May God lift you up and out of
your dead places with loving arms and breathe into
you hope and life beyond measure. Held by the hand
of God, may you see your life in a new way and with
new possibilities — with the eyes of the Creator who
sees the whole of you and loves it unconditionally.
May the God of VITALITY bless you.

numbness

PARDON

revenge

May you find God's
blessing when everything
in you wants *revenge* and
retribution for the evil done
by another, when your impulse
is to retaliate and your need is to be
vindicated. At those times may you be blessed with
a longer reach into the depths of your soul. May you
find your vindication in the strength that is gained
through your faithfulness to God's mercy and your
"payback" in the peace that is known in forgiveness.
May the God of PARDON bless you.

ACCORD

May God bless you
in your discord, when
instability invades your
day and throws you into
moments of uneasiness and
agitation. May God catch you in those
moments and carry you back to the center of your
soul, the dwelling place of God, where calm and
stillness live. May you know there the freedom of
being known and loved unconditionally. May the
God of ACCORD bless you.

instability

HEALING PRESENCE

brokenness

May God bless you
with healing presence
when you are *broken*. When
your will and your passion
are rendered useless by the
circumstances of your life, may you look
to God to restore you. May you return to the union
with God that was there at your creation and may
God bring you back to wholeness. In the fullness of
God's presence may you reclaim your purpose and
call. May the God of HEALING PRESENCE bless you.

90

GENTLE TRUTH

May you be made holy
when you experience
your own *dishonesty,*
when departure from what is
true and just leads you to a place
of uneasiness and disquiet. From that
place may God gently guide you to a realization of
the truth planted deep within you. May you claim
that truth, its power to transform you and its desire
to free you for peace. May the God of GENTLE TRUTH
bless you.

dishonesty

WHOLENESS

May you be blessed
when you experience
yourself as incomplete
and *needy,* when you set
your sights on what is outside
you to find wholeness. At those times
may you shift your vision inward where God has a
permanent dwelling. As you reach your hand inward
may you receive the alms that God offers there: grace
to transform you, gifts to complete you, and serenity to
make you whole. May the God of WHOLENESS bless you.

PARENT GOD

May you know blessing
when you find yourself
orphaned by the death of a
parent or the diminishment of
the generation before you. When
you are left to your own devices and find
yourself responsible for your own future, may you hear
the voice of God in your inmost being: "I will not leave
you orphaned." May you know this parent God beside
you and before you, guiding and loving you into a future
of justice, peace, and compassion for all who feel alone
in this world. May the PARENT GOD bless you.

orphan

93

ENLIGHTENMENT

division

May God bring you
to blessing when you
struggle with a life that
is *divided* and separated
from itself, when fear, dread,
and embarrassment keep parts of you
hidden in the shadows. May God shine the light of
compassion into those unseen places to reveal to
you the glimpses of glory that lie just beneath the
surface of hurt or shame. May you be transformed by
your faithfulness to the shadows and may the God of
ENLIGHTENMENT bless you.

TRANSFORMATION

May you be made holy
when you are overcome
by the effects of *abuse* ... of
mind, soul, body, or spirit. May
your journey into the experience
bring you to its other side where
compassion awaits you and peace stands ready to
welcome you home to yourself. May God bless you
with all that you need to be faithful to the process.
And may your faithfulness open you to look for inner
strength and wisdom even in the pain. May the God
of TRANSFORMATION give you strength and bless you.

abuse

95

RE-UNION

May God look upon you
and bless you when you
become *widowed,* when you
are left alone and without the
companionship of a soul mate. At
the times when your loneliness is most
acute, may you be blessed with the overwhelming
awareness of God's arms linking you once again in an
embrace that will never end. In your desire for reunion
may you know the intensity of God's desire to be One
with you. May the God of RE-UNION bless you.

RECONCILIATION

May God bless you and
make you holy through
the pain of *estrangement*
and alienation from those you
love. When emotional distance
hinders relationships, may you be graced
with the ability to see across the distance with the
eyes of God. When wounded sensitivities interfere
may you love with God's compassion, gently
carrying all into a place of healing. May the God of
RECONCILIATION bless you.

estrangement

SELF-TRUST

doubt

May you be blessed by
God when you *doubt
yourself,* when you are
unsure about the decisions
you've made or the direction in
which you are going. May you be blessed
with the grace to trust the God who partners with you
and is working in you. This is the God who loves you
and knows you as God's own work of art. This is the
God who transforms even bad choices into gifts for
those who are faithful. May the God of SELF-TRUST
bless you.

GRATEFUL REST

May you find blessing
when you feel *hurried*
and rushed in your life and
time seems to be at a premium.
May you experience God's
presence in your haste, encouraging you
and energizing you as you do the work of justice
and peace, of compassion and prophecy. And when
rest does come may you reflect on and remember
what you and God have done together and be filled
with gratitude. Then may the God of GRATEFUL REST
bless you.

hurry

FAITHFUL: SUPPORT

pressure

May God make
you holy when you
feel pressured by the
circumstances or expectations
that surround you. May you
experience the lightness in your step
that comes with knowing that God walks with you.
May you be blessed with the grace to share your
burdens with your God who carries the load on broad
shoulders and offers relief in his total love for you
and companionship with you. May God, FAITHFUL:
SUPPORT, bless you.

SPIRIT OF GOD

May you be
blessed when you feel
unprepared or unqualified
for the task at hand and fear
begins to take over your spirit.
May it be then that you allow God's Spirit
to take over your fear. May you step aside and leave
room for God to fill in the spaces and the gaps.
Then, having granted God entry, may you rejoice as
you watch God work in you and through you and
even around you. May the SPIRIT OF GOD grace you
and bless you.

unpreparedness

LIBERATION

dis-ability

May God make you holy
in your *dis-ability*.
When life's circumstances and
surprises immobilize and hinder
you, may you be opened to the
realization that God is supremely able to
compensate with greater gifts than you can imagine.
May you recognize those gifts within you and may
they be the source of hope and liberation for you and
for all those with whom you share them. May God,
LIBERATOR, bless you.

GIFTING GOD

May you be made holy
when you are feeling
heavy with anxiety and
overweight in mind, soul, body,
or spirit. May the weight of your
distress melt away when you come to the
realization that your God loves you without condition
and calls you far beyond those weighty concerns to
discover the sacred gifts within you. May you come
to value those gifts and allow them to set you on the
path to your true self where God and you are One.
May you be blessed over and over by this GIFTING GOD.

heaviness

VOICE OF GOD

uncertainty

May God stand with you when you are *uncertain* and don't know which way to turn, leaving you unsure of your path. At those times may you sense God standing beside you, longing for your happiness and gently nudging you toward your truth. May you enter the place within you that hears this God and leads you to that deep-down knowing even in the midst of uncertainty. May the VOICE OF GOD lead you and bless you.

AUTHENTICITY

May you know blessing
when you have been
misjudged or when your
words or intentions have
been misconstrued or mistaken.
May you settle into that place within
you that is filled with truth and authenticity and
may you find there your true intent and your most
authentic meaning. May you also find the words that
will transform perceptions and invite reconciliation
among those who people your life. May the God of
AUTHENTICITY bless you.

misjudging

105

TIME

May you find blessing
when you experience
burnout and all your
resources seem to be used up
and your reserves depleted. When
you are reduced to your core, may you
discover there the image of God who loves you and
receives you even in your emptiness. May you be
blessed with time to gaze upon God's image in you
and be replenished and brought back to life by what
God has planted deep within you. May the God of TIME
bless you.

ENCOURAGEMENT

May God be with
you when you are
discouraged and your
hope and anticipation are
diminished by the circumstances
of the life around you. At those times
may you set your sights on the passion that God
has awakened within you and may you draw
courage from it. May your embrace of God's dream
once again fire that passion in you. May the God of
ENCOURAGEMENT bless you.

discouragement

HOPEFULNESS

May God stand with you when you find yourself *unemployed* and seemingly useless, when discouragement overtakes and pummels your reasons for hope. May the God standing with you be your protection, believing in and reminding you always of the gifts that are yours and the love with which they have been given and shared. In this remembering may you find a place of optimism and anticipation in your life. May the God of HOPEFULNESS bless you.

GRATITUDE

May you be made
holy when you discover
within yourself the place
of *envy* where the gifts of
others bring you to sadness. As
you contemplate what it is you desire
for yourself, may your heart be drawn to what God
desires for you. May you become so consumed with
gratitude for the gifts you have been given and the
gift that you are that you are brought to a genuine
enthusiasm for the gifts of others. May the God of
GRATITUDE bless you.

envy

REDEMPTION

cynicism

May you discover
God's blessing when
you become sarcastic or
cynical of the world around
you, when the level of your trust
in the sincerity of others is at its lowest.
May God first sit with you in the hurt places that have
led to your distrust and then may God speak healing
words through you to break the patterns of distrust
and to build up a restored community around you.
May the GOD WHO REDEEMS bless you.

INDEX

INDEX

INDEX

INDEX

INDEX

INDEX